C000062359

Year 5

Excellence in Problem Solving Mathematics

Hilary Koll and Steve Mills

RISING ★ STARS

Rising Stars UK Ltd.

7 Hatchers Mews, Bermondsey Street, London, SE1 3GS

www.risingstars-uk.com

Published 2010

Authors: Hilary Koll and Steve Mills

Design and typesetting: Sally Boothroyd

Editorial: Bruce Nicholson, Ruth Burns

Artwork: Sally Boothroyd, Michael Emmerson, David Woodroffe

Cover Design: Words and Pictures

Photo acknowledgements
p.11 *pineapple* © Jiri Miklo /iStockphoto; **p.23** *flags* © Hanquan Chen/iStockphoto, *games console* © Adam Filipowicz/iStockphoto; **p.29** *football shirt* Mark Wragg/iStockphoto; **p.35** *presents* © Aldo Murillo/iStockphoto; **p.37** *orange juice* © Pali Rao/iStockphoto; **p.39** *train* © hfn/iStockphoto; **p.41** *polyhedron art* © Andrew Cribb/iStockphoto; **p.43** *knotted rope* © Zoran Kolundzija/iStockphoto

British Library Cataloguing in Publication Data.

A CIP record for this book is available from the British Library.

ISBN: 978-1-84680-763-3

Printed by Craft Print International Ltd, Singapore.

Contents

	Using and applying mathematics					Counting and understanding number					Knowing and using number facts			
	Solve one- and two-step problems involving whole numbers and decimals and all four operations, choosing and using appropriate calculation strategies, including calculator use	Represent a puzzle or problem by identifying and recording the information or calculations needed to solve it; find possible solutions and confirm them in the context of the problem	Plan and pursue an enquiry; present evidence by collecting, organising and interpreting information; suggest extensions to the enquiry	Explore patterns, properties and relationships and propose a general statement involving numbers or shapes; identify examples for which the statement is true or false	Explain reasoning using diagrams, graphs and text; refine ways of recording using images and symbols	Count from any given number in whole-number and decimal steps, extending beyond zero when counting backwards; relate the numbers to their position on a number line	Explain what each digit represents in whole numbers and decimals with up to two places, and partition, round and order these numbers	Express a smaller whole number as a fraction of a larger one, e.g. recognise that 5 out of 8 is $\frac{5}{8}$; find equivalent fractions, e.g. $\frac{7}{10} = \frac{14}{20}$, or $\frac{19}{100} = \frac{19}{10}$; relate fractions to their decimal representations	Understand percentage as the number of parts in every 100 and express tenths and hundredths as percentages	Use sequences to scale numbers up or down; solve problems involving proportions of quantities, e.g. decrease quantities in a recipe designed to feed six people	Use knowledge of place value and addition and subtraction of two-digit numbers to derive sums and differences, doubles and halves of decimals, e.g. 6.5 ± 2.7, halve 5.6, double 0.34	Recall quickly multiplication facts up to 10 × 10 and use them to multiply pairs of multiples of 10 and 100; derive quickly corresponding division facts	Identify pairs of factors of two-digit whole numbers and find common multiples, e.g. for 6 and 9	Use knowledge of rounding, place value, number facts and inverse operations to estimate and check calculations
Sequences	✔	✔		✔	✔	✔								
Mixed calculations (1)	✔	✔		✔	✔						✔	✔		✔
Mixed calculations (2)	✔	✔		✔	✔						✔	✔		✔
Fractions	✔	✔		✔	✔			✔	✔	✔			✔	
Decimals	✔	✔		✔	✔		✔	✔	✔					
Percentages	✔	✔		✔	✔				✔					
Equivalence	✔	✔		✔	✔			✔	✔	✔				
Ratio	✔	✔		✔	✔			✔		✔				
Place value	✔	✔		✔	✔		✔							✔
Money	✔	✔		✔	✔		✔				✔			✔
Negative numbers	✔	✔		✔	✔	✔								
Reading scales	✔	✔		✔	✔	✔								
Measures (1)	✔	✔		✔	✔						✔	✔		✔
Measures (2)	✔	✔		✔	✔						✔	✔		✔
Time	✔	✔		✔	✔									
2-D and 3-D shapes	✔	✔		✔	✔									
Angles	✔	✔		✔	✔									
Data handling	✔	✔	✔	✔	✔									

Calculating

- Extend mental methods for whole-number calculations, e.g. to multiply a two-digit number by a one-digit number (e.g. 12 × 9), to multiply by 25 (e.g. 16 × 25), to subtract one near multiple of 1000 from another (e.g. 6070 – 4097)
- Use efficient written methods to add and subtract whole numbers and decimals with up to two decimal places
- Use understanding of place value to multiply and divide whole numbers and decimals by 10, 100 or 1000
- Refine and use efficient written methods to multiply and divide HTU × U, TU × TU, U.t × U, and HTU ÷ U
- Find fractions using division, e.g. $\frac{1}{100}$ of 5 kg, and percentages of numbers and quantities, e.g. 10%, 5% and 15% of £80
- Use a calculator to solve problems, including those involving decimals or fractions, e.g. to find $\frac{3}{4}$ of 150 g; interpret the display correctly in the context of measurement

Understanding shape

- Vldentify, visualise and describe properties of rectangles, triangles, regular polygons and 3-D solids; use knowledge of properties to draw 2-D shapes and identify and draw nets of 3-D shapes
- Read and plot coordinates in the first quadrant; recognise parallel and perpendicular lines in grids and shapes; use a set-square and ruler to draw shapes with perpendicular or parallel sides
- Complete patterns with up to two lines of symmetry and draw the position of a shape after a reflection or translation
- Estimate, draw and measure acute and obtuse angles using an angle measurer or protractor to a suitable degree of accuracy; calculate angles in a straight line

Measuring

- Read, choose, use and record standard metric units to estimate and measure length, weight and capacity to a suitable degree of accuracy, e.g. the nearest centimetre; convert larger to smaller units using decimals to one place, e.g. change 2.6 kg to 2600 g
- Interpret a reading that lies between two unnumbered divisions on a scale
- Draw and measure lines to the nearest millimetre; measure and calculate the perimeter of regular and irregular polygons; use the formula for the area of a rectangle to calculate its area
- Read timetables and time using 24-hour clock notation; use a calendar to calculate time intervals

Handling data

- Describe the occurrence of familiar events using the language of chance or likelihood
- Answer a set of related questions by collecting, selecting and organising relevant data; draw conclusions, using ICT to present features, and identify further questions to ask
- Construct frequency tables, pictograms and bar and line graphs to represent the frequencies of events and changes over time
- Find and interpret the mode of a set of data

How to use this book

This book is designed to help you use your mathematical skills to solve a range of problems, many of which are written in words rather than figures.

Rather than giving a calculation like:

$$4 \times 6 = \boxed{}$$

a word problem might be something like:

If I have 4 six-packs of cola, how many cans of cola do I have in total?

The answer is the same, but you need to think about it a bit more and remember to answer by writing or saying: *I have 24 cans of cola in total.*

The example problem

The flow chart takes you through an example problem step-by-step. This is important when answering word problems as it helps you to order your thoughts, do each part of the problem in the right order and check your work!

Every problem has the same five steps:

READ the question, then read it again

DECIDE your operations and units

APPROXIMATE your answer

CALCULATE

CHECK your answer

We can remember this by using this mnemonic:

Rain

Drops

Are

Crystal

Clear

The introduction

This section of each page gives you an idea of the sort of problems you are likely to see and helps you to understand what maths you need to use.

2-D and 3-D shapes

When solving 2-D and 3-D shape problems you need to remember the names of common shapes and their properties, such as how many sides, faces, edges, vertices (corners), or right angles or lines of symmetry they have.

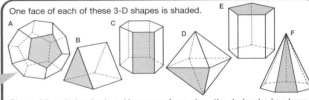

One face of each of these 3-D shapes is shaded.

Shape A is a dodecahedron. How many faces does the dodecahedron have, what is the name of the shape of the shaded face and is the shaded face regular or not?

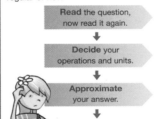

Read the question, now read it again.	Read slowly and carefully. You are being asked three questions.
Decide your operations and units.	I need to count the faces and work out what shape the shaded face is, including whether it is regular or not.
Approximate your answer.	I'll imagine I was holding this shape in my hands.
Calculate.	I think the shape has 12 faces. The shaded face has five equal sides and five equal angles so it is a regular pentagon.
Check.	I'll check that I've answered all parts of the question.

40

Hints and tips

The Hints and tips section gives you useful ideas for completing the problems on the opposite page. These are the things you need to remember if you are doing a quiz or test.

The questions

The questions get harder as you go down the page.

- Section 1 questions are fairly straightforward and help you to practise your skills.

- Section 2 questions are a bit harder. They will help you to remember all the key points.

2-D AND 3-D SHAPES

Hints and tips

A regular 2-D shape is one that has equal sides and equal angles. A regular triangle is called an equilateral triangle.

Questions

1 a) Shape D is a tetrahedron. How many faces does the tetrahedron have, what is the name of the shape of the shaded face and is the shaded face regular or not?

b) Look at shape B. What is the name of the 3-D shape? Two of its faces are triangles, what are the names of the shapes of the other faces and how many are there?

2 a) Fin chooses one of the shapes shown. It has a face that is a regular hexagon. Which shape is it and what is the name of its shaded face?

b) A shape is made from the following faces: one regular quadrilateral and four equilateral triangles. What is the name of the shape?

CHALLENGE! Look around you and find boxes and objects that are different 3-D shapes. Make a list of these shapes, the shapes of their faces and their properties. E.g.:

A Toblerone bar is a triangular prism, with two faces that are equilateral triangles and three rectangular faces. The rectangles are not regular.

Challenge

The Challenge is really tough and sometimes involves making up games and your own questions.

Explore

3-D shapes that have all straight edges are known as **polyhedrons**. These shapes appear in lots of computer-generated art. Go to **Google images** and search for 'polyhedron art' and choose your favourite images. You could try drawing your own designs or could copy your favourites.

41

Explore

This section gives you a chance to investigate the topic in more depth and to make links with other subjects. You may be asked to write about something or do some research.

Ten top tips for working with word problems

1 *Work step-by-step.* Follow the flow chart.

Rain — **Read** the question, now read it again.

⬇

Drops — **Decide** your operations and units.

⬇

Are — **Approximate** your answer.

⬇

Crystal — **Calculate.**

⬇

Clear — **Check.**

2 Always *show your working* or 'method'. This will help you to keep track of what you have done and may help you to get extra marks.

3 Always *include the units* in your answer. If you don't, you won't get full marks.

4 When you first read through a question, *underline important words and numbers*. This will help you to remember the important bits.

5 *Draw a picture to help you.* Sometimes a question is easier if you can 'see' it. For example, drawing 6 apples can help you if you need to divide them.

6 If the problem has a number of steps, break it down and do *one step at a time*.

7 To *check your answers*, look at the inverse operation.

8 Sometimes an answer will 'sound right'. Read it out (quietly) and listen. *Does it make sense?*

9 If you are using measurements (grams, litres, cm), make sure that the *units are the same* before you calculate.

10 Once again! *Read the question again and check that your solution answers it.*

Sequences

Most sequences go up or down in equal-sized steps. Find the difference between adjacent numbers to work out the step size and then count on, or back, to find the missing numbers in the sequence.

Jo has a 'lift-the-flap' puzzle book.
The sequence goes up in equal steps.
Which numbers are underneath the flaps?

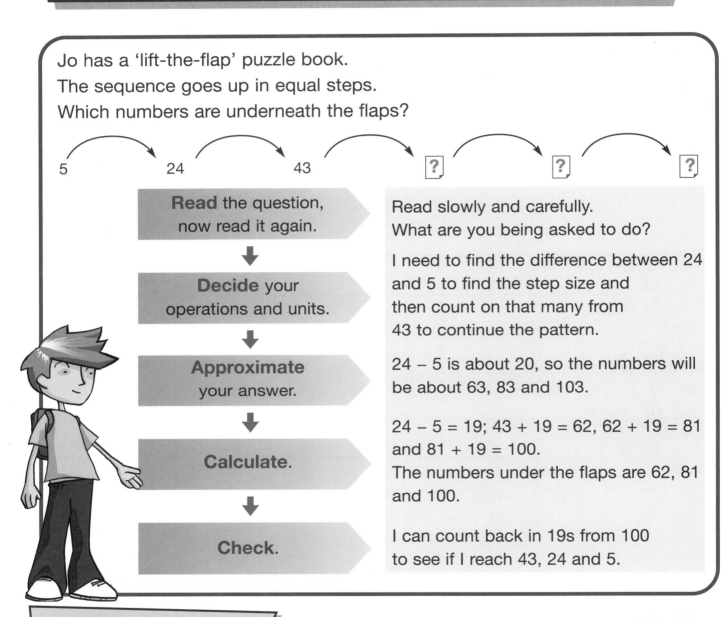

5   24   43   ?   ?   ?

Read the question, now read it again.

⬇

Decide your operations and units.

⬇

Approximate your answer.

⬇

Calculate.

⬇

Check.

Read slowly and carefully. What are you being asked to do?

I need to find the difference between 24 and 5 to find the step size and then count on that many from 43 to continue the pattern.

24 – 5 is about 20, so the numbers will be about 63, 83 and 103.

24 – 5 = 19; 43 + 19 = 62, 62 + 19 = 81 and 81 + 19 = 100.
The numbers under the flaps are 62, 81 and 100.

I can count back in 19s from 100 to see if I reach 43, 24 and 5.

Hints and tips

If counting on, or back, in decimal steps, e.g. in steps of 0.3 from 1.2, treat them as if they were whole numbers, such as counting on in 3s from 12. Then put the decimal points in the correct places.

Questions

1 Which numbers are under the flaps?

a)

5 → 23 → 41 → [?] → [?] → 95

b)

88 → 71 → 54 → [?] → [?] → 3

c)

8 → 21 → 34 → [?] → [?] → [?]

2 Find the missing numbers in these sequences.

a)

5.6 → 4.8 → 4.0 → [?] → [?] → 1.6

b)

0.3 → [?] → [?] → [?] → 3.1 → 3.8

CHALLENGE! Make up three different number sequences of your own that start with the number 37 and have the number 70 somewhere in the sequence.

37
70

Explore

Look in books or on the Internet to find out about a special sequence called the 'Fibonacci sequence'. It is a pattern that does not go up in equal step sizes, but it is a sequence that is found in many real-life situations. Can you find out how pineapples and some plant leaves are related to this sequence?

Mixed calculations (1)

It is important to be able to work out whether to add, subtract, multiply or divide to find the answer to a word problem.

A plane has 40 rows of seats. In each row there are two seats, then four seats and then two seats as shown in this diagram.

If passengers are sitting in all except 19 of the seats on the plane, how many passengers are there?

Read the question, now read it again.

Decide your operations and units.

Approximate your answer.

Calculate.

Check.

Read slowly and carefully.
What is the important information?

I need to add 2, 4 and 2 to find the number of seats in each row and then multiply this by 40. Finally, I'll subtract 19 from this number.

$8 \times 40 - 19$ is about $320 - 20$, so the answer will be about 300.

$8 \times 40 = 320$; $320 - 19 = 301$, so the answer is 301 passengers.

I can add 19 to 301 and then divide by 8 to see if I get 40 rows.

Hints and tips

Use a mental or written method to do your calculations. Always write the answer clearly, giving the unit if necessary. Then make sure you read through the question again to check whether the answer makes sense.

Questions

 1

a) There are 1019 passengers at a Greek airport about to fly to London, Manchester or Birmingham. There are 293 going to London and 368 going to Manchester. How many are going to Birmingham?

b) A plane has 248 seats, of which 67 are empty and 8 are being used by the airline staff. The rest of the seats are taken by passengers. How many passengers are there?

c) Of the 338 passengers on a plane, 179 are men, 152 are women and the rest are children. How many passengers are children?

2

a) A plane has 38 rows. The front 10 rows each have 6 seats and the rest of the rows have 8 seats. How many seats are there in total?

b) On a flight to New York, there are 37 children and 6 times as many adults. If there are 348 seats on the plane, how many are empty?

c) A plane has 448 seats. If the seats are in equal-sized rows and there are 32 rows, how many seats are there in each row?

CHALLENGE!

When booking a flight, you pay airport taxes on top of the ticket price. Using this price list, write three questions of your own about the information for a partner to answer.

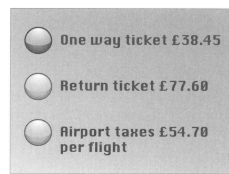

One way ticket £38.45

Return ticket £77.60

Airport taxes £54.70 per flight

Explore

Can you name the continents of the world? Choose a capital city from each continent. Use the Internet and try to find out how long a flight to each city would take from London.

Mixed calculations (2)

It is important to be able to work out whether to add, subtract, multiply or divide, or to do a combination of these, to find the answer to a word problem.

In a TV talent show, the number of telephone votes from viewers and the number of votes from the people in the studio audience are added together for the final count. Claudia's final count is 4492 votes. One quarter of the votes are from the studio audience. How many are telephone votes?

Read the question, now read it again.	Read slowly and carefully. Which are the important numbers?
	I need to find one quarter of 4492 and subtract the answer from 4492 to find the number of telephone votes. I can find one quarter by dividing by 4.
Decide your operations and units.	
Approximate your answer.	$4000 \div 4 = 1000$, $4000 - 1000 = 3000$, so the answer will be about 3000.
Calculate.	$4492 \div 4 = 1123$, $4492 - 1123 = 3369$, so there are 3369 telephone votes.
Check.	$3369 + 1123 = 4492$. Yes, I was correct!

Hints and tips

Sometimes it is useful to draw a diagram to help you work through a complicated question. E.g. if there are three people you could draw three stick people and note the information about them by the drawings to help you work out what to do.

Questions

1 a) One talent act, Mick the Magician, has a total of 6630 votes. One-tenth of the votes are from the studio audience and the rest are from telephone votes. How many are telephone votes?

b) A TV talent show has an audience of 964. Of the audience 272 are children, 469 are women and the rest are men. How many are men?

2 a) Sam has three times the number of votes that Raz has. If Raz had half as many votes as Jo and Jo has 376 votes, how many votes does Sam have?

b) Ali gets 462 votes in Week 1 and four times as many votes in Week 2. In Week 3 he gets 375 more than in Week 2. How many votes does he get in Week 3?

CHALLENGE! This chart shows the number of votes for some talent show contestants. Write three questions about the table for a partner to answer. Remember to work out the answers too!

Contestant	Studio votes	Telephone votes	Total votes
Kallum	4035	508	
Sam	3986	962	
Ali	5146	245	

Explore

Write a story about entering a talent contest. Imagine how you would feel as you were performing. Write about the other contestants and describe how the contest went, including numbers of votes from the studio audience and by telephone.

Fractions

For fraction problems you may be asked to find fractions of numbers, for example, one-quarter or two-fifths of a number or to give a fraction of a whole.

This picture shows 20 people. Look carefully at the picture. What proportion of the people are wearing trousers? Give your answer as a fraction in its simplest form.

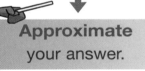

Read the question, now read it again.

⬇

Decide your operations and units.

⬇

Approximate your answer.

⬇

Calculate.

⬇

Check.

The question is asking me what fraction of the 20 people are wearing trousers.

I'll count the number that wear trousers (that's the numerator). The denominator will be 20 as there are 20 people in total. Finally, I'll change the fraction to its simplest form by dividing.

There are 15 people in trousers, so that's $\frac{15}{20}$.

$\frac{15}{20}$ – I'll divide the numerator and denominator by 5 to get $\frac{3}{4}$.

I can check that $\frac{3}{4}$ of 20 is 15. Yes, I was correct!

Hints and tips

When changing a fraction to its simplest form, divide the **numerator** (the number on the top) and the **denominator** (the number on the bottom) *by the same number* to get whole number answers. Keep doing this until you can't do this anymore.

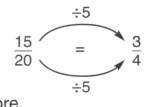

$$\frac{15}{20} \xrightarrow[\div 5]{\div 5} = \frac{3}{4}$$

Questions

1 a) Look at the picture opposite. What proportion of the people are female? Give your answer as a fraction in its simplest form.

b) What proportion of the people are wearing hats? Give your answer as a fraction in its simplest form.

c) What proportion of the people are wearing shorts? Give your answer as a fraction in its simplest form.

2 a) There are 24 people on a catwalk. Of those, 16 are wearing sunglasses. What proportion of them are wearing sunglasses? Give your answer in its simplest form.

b) There are 96 people watching a catwalk show. Of these, 84 of these people are women. What proportion of them are women? Give your answer in its simplest form.

CHALLENGE. Write some proportion questions about people on a catwalk for a partner to answer. Don't forget to work out the answers too!

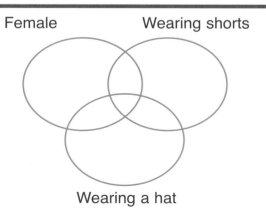

Explore

Copy this Venn diagram onto a large piece of paper. Draw some pictures of different people that could be sorted into each section of the diagram.

Female   Wearing shorts

Wearing a hat

Decimals

Decimals are ways of showing parts of whole numbers, using a decimal point, for example, 3.5 kg, 0.1 km, etc. You need to know that the first digit after the decimal point stands for tenths and the second stands for hundredths.

Eva Lot and Jim Muscle are weightlifters in a competition. In Round 1, Eva lifts 43.45 kg and Jim lifts 43.9 kg. Who lifts the most and by how much?

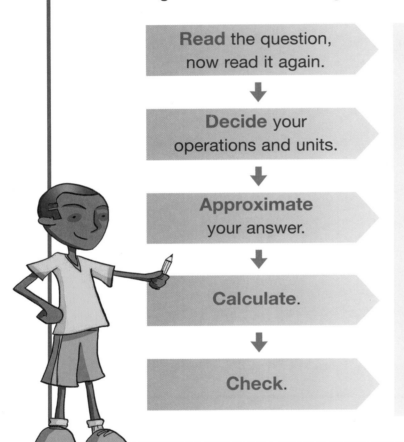

Read the question, now read it again.

⬇

Decide your operations and units.

⬇

Approximate your answer.

⬇

Calculate.

⬇

Check.

Read carefully. Write the important numbers and their units.

I need to say if 43.45 is larger or smaller than 43.9. Then I'll subtract the smaller from the larger number.

I'll make sure both decimals have the same number of digits after the decimal point (43.45 and 43.90) to make them easier to compare.

43.90 kg is larger than 43.45 kg and 43.90 kg − 43.45 kg = 0.45 kg. So Jim lifts 0.45 kg more than Eva.

I can add 0.45 kg to 43.45 kg to check it is 43.90 kg. Yes, it is!

Hints and tips

Remember that the digits to the right of the decimal point are part numbers and those to the left are whole numbers.

t is tenths, so 0.6 means 6 tenths or $\frac{6}{10}$.

h is hundredths, so 0.05 is 5 hundredths or $\frac{5}{100}$.

U	.	t	h
7	.	6	5

Questions

1 a) In Round 2, Eva lifts 45.8 kg
and Jim lifts 45.75 kg.
Who lifts the most and by
how much?

  b) In Round 3, Jim adds an extra two 0.3 kg weights onto
his original weight of 45.75 kg. What is the total weight now?

  c) Eva lifts 9 × 5 kg weights, plus 3 × 0.2 kg weights, plus one
0.05 kg weight. What is the total weight she lifts?

2 a) Here are the weights that five other weightlifters manage to lift.
Put the weights in order of size, starting with the lightest.

85.6 kg   86 kg   85.35 kg   85.62 kg   85.06 kg

  b) Ivor, Eva and Jim all take part in a competition. Ivor lifts three
times the weight Eva lifts and Jim lifts twice as much as Eva.
If Jim lifts 87 kg, how much do Eva and Ivor each lift?

CHALLENGE.

The greater than (>) and less than (<) signs
can be used to show which weights are
heavier or lighter, e.g. 46.8 kg > 46.72 kg.
Write six different statements including
< or > using the decimals on this page.

Explore

Did you know that if you put a kilogram weight on
some weighing scales on the Moon, it would not show one kilogram?
It would be six times lighter! If you stood on the scales, they would show
a different mass on the Moon than on Earth. Find out why this happens.
How much would you weigh on the Moon or on other planets? Go to
www.exploratorium.edu/ronh/weight to find out.

Percentages

Percent means 'out of a hundred'. Percentages are another way to show fractions with the denominator 100, e.g. $\frac{4}{100} = 4\%$, $\frac{58}{100} = 58\%$. When solving percentage problems, start with a fraction, then change it to have the denominator 100.

On an online shopping site, people selling items (sellers) are scored positively or negatively. Their 'rating' is the number of positive scores out of the total number of scores, given as a percentage.

Seller	Positive scores	Total scores	Percentage rating
gr8seller	7	10	70%
goods4u	73	100	
buyfromme	6	10	
abigcon	44	50	
supasell	12	50	
gd@value	20	25	
Gr8guy	19	20	

What is the rating for 'abigcon' as a percentage?

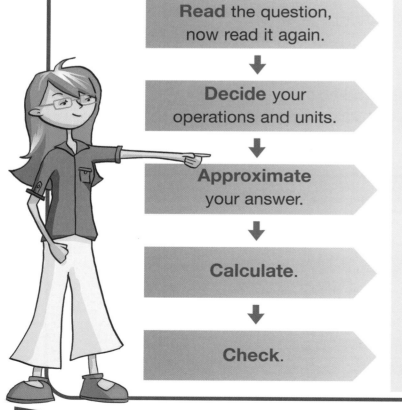

Read the question, now read it again.

Read slowly and carefully. What is the table showing?

Decide your operations and units.

I need to write 44 out of 50 as a fraction with the denominator 100, and then write this as a percentage.

Approximate your answer.

$\frac{44}{50}$ is more than three-quarters, so the percentage will be over 75%.

Calculate.

$\frac{44}{50} = \frac{88}{100}$, so the answer is 88%.

Check.

I could use a calculator to divide 44 by 50 and then multiply the decimal by 100 to get the percentage. Yes, it's 88%!

Hints and tips

To help you work out a percentage, think of a score as a fraction first, e.g. $\frac{7}{10}$ or $\frac{27}{100}$. Remember that one-tenth is equivalent to 10% and two-tenths is equivalent to 20%.

Questions

1 a) Look at the table opposite. What is the rating for 'buyfromme' as a percentage?

b) What is the rating for 'goods4u' as a percentage?

c) What is the rating for 'supasell' as a percentage?

2 a) Another seller has four positive scores out of a total of five scores. What is his percentage rating?

b) What is the difference between the percentage ratings of 'gr8seller' and 'gd@value'?

c) What is the difference between the percentage ratings of 'abigcon' and 'Gr8guy'?

CHALLENGE! Go to a website that has reviews of films, such as **www.rottentomatoes.com**. Look at the percentage scores for films you have watched and find out how many people voted and how many of the votes were positive (fresh). Can you work out how many people thought the film was bad (rotten)?

Explore

Look at some clothes labels. Can you see any percentages? What does it mean if a label says '90% cotton'? What do you notice if you add up all the percentages on a label? Write some notes about what you find out.

Equivalence

Equivalence means 'has the same value as'. A fraction such as $\frac{1}{2}$ has the same value as the decimal 0.5 and the percentage 50%, so we say that $\frac{1}{2}$, 0.5 and 50% are equivalent.

These flags are from different countries. They are all the same size.

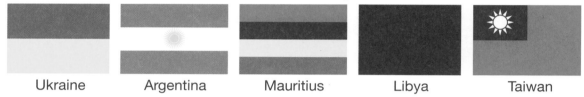

Ukraine   Argentina   Mauritius   Libya   Taiwan

What proportion of Argentina's flag is blue? Give your answer as a fraction, as a decimal and as a percentage, rounding if necessary.

Read the question, now read it again.

⬇

Decide your operations and units.

⬇

Approximate your answer.

⬇

Calculate.

⬇

Check.

I must find the proportion as a fraction, decimal and percentage.

I will first decide what fraction is blue and then convert this to a decimal and then a percentage by writing the fraction out of 100.

Two out of three equal parts are blue, which is two-thirds ($\frac{2}{3}$).

$\frac{2}{3}$ is about $\frac{67}{100}$, which is about 0.67 or 67%.

I'll read the question again and make sure my answer makes sense. Yes, I was correct!

Hints and tips

Remember these equivalents:

$\frac{1}{2} = 0.5 = 50\%$	$\frac{1}{10} = 0.1 = 10\%$	$\frac{1}{100} = 0.01 = 1\%$	$\frac{1}{3} \approx 0.33 \approx 33\%$
$\frac{1}{4} = 0.25 = 25\%$	$\frac{2}{10} = 0.2 = 20\%$	$\frac{2}{100} = 0.02 = 2\%$	$\frac{2}{3} \approx 0.67 \approx 67\%$
$\frac{3}{4} = 0.75 = 75\%$	and so on	and so on	

Questions

1 a) Look at the flags opposite. What proportion of Taiwan's flag is red? Give your answer as a fraction, as a decimal and as a percentage.

b) What proportion of the Mauritian flag is green? Give your answer as a fraction, as a decimal and as a percentage.

c) How many times the size is the amount of yellow on the Ukrainian flag than the amount of yellow on the Mauritian flag?

2 a) The Mauritian and Taiwanese flags are laid side by side so that they touch. What proportion of the two flags is red? Give your answer as a fraction, as a decimal and as a percentage.

b) The Mauritian and Libyan flags are laid side by side so that they touch. What proportion of the two flags is green? Give your answer as a fraction.

c) The French flag has one-third red, one-third blue and the rest is white. Approximately what percentage is white?

CHALLENGE!

About $\frac{1}{6}$ of the South African flag is red. Can you work out approximately what percentage this is? You could use a calculator to divide the numerator by the denominator to find out.

Explore

Find out about flags of other countries and see what proportions are different colours. Can you find two countries that have different flags, but where both flags are about 67% red and the other colour is white? Which country's flag has the proportions of $\frac{5}{9}$ blue and $\frac{4}{9}$ white?

Ratio

Ratio is the relationship between two or more quantities, for example, the amounts of blackcurrant to water in a juice drink, or the numbers of boys and girls in a class.

At Fred's party, the ratio of boys to girls is 2:3, which means two boys to every three girls. If there are 12 boys at the party, how many girls are there?

Read the question, now read it again.

Decide your operations and units.

Approximate your answer.

Calculate.

Check.

Read slowly. Write the ratio and the headings, with the other important number under the right heading.

Boys	:	Girls
2	:	3
12	:	?

I need to find what to multiply 2 by to get 12 and then do the same to 3 to get the number of girls.

There are more girls than boys, so the number of girls will be greater than 12.

I multiply 2 by 6 to get 12, so I must multiply 3 by 6 to get the answer. $3 \times 6 = 18$, so there are 18 girls.

I can check that both numbers (12 and 18) can be divided by the same number (6) to get the numbers in the initial ratio, 2 and 3. Yes!

Hints and tips

When working out ratios, remember that both numbers in a ratio must be multiplied by the same number to get an equivalent ratio, for example:

Boys : Girls
×6 ⟨ 2 : 3 ⟩ ×6
12 : 18

Questions

1

a) At Chloe's party, the ratio of boys to girls is 2:5.
If there are 8 boys at the party, how many girls are there?

b) At Leroy's party, the ratio of boys to girls is 3:1.
If there are 6 girls at the party, how many boys are there?

c) At Ben's party, the ratio of boys to girls is 4:3.
If there are 12 boys at the party, how many girls are there?

2

a) There are 24 children at a party. The ratio of boys to girls is 5:1.
How many are boys and how many are girls?

b) There are 28 children at a party. The ratio of boys to girls is 3:4.
How many are boys and how many are girls?

CHALLENGE!

These ratios are all equivalent:

2:3   4:6   6:9   8:12   10:15   12:18   14:21

Write a family of ratios that are equivalent to the ratio 4:5.

Explore

People all around the world have parties for different
reasons. Find out about the festival of Diwali. You could go to
www.kidsgen.com/events and click on this, or other celebrations, to find
out more. Make a leaflet about what you find out.

Place value

When solving place value problems, you might be asked to add, subtract, multiply or divide multiples of 10, 100 or 1000, such as 60, 400, or 3000.

Alfie is playing a computer game. In Round 1 he scores 400 points and in Round 2 he scores 20 times more than in Round 1. How many did he score in Rounds 1 and 2 together?

Read the question, now read it again.	Read slowly and carefully and make a note of the numbers.
Decide your operations and units.	I must multiply 400 by 20 and then add the answer to 400.
Approximate your answer.	400 × 2 would be 800, so the answer will be 10 times larger, plus 400.
Calculate.	400 × 20 = 4 × 2 × 100 × 10 = 8 × 1000 = 8000. Finally, I must add 8000 + 400 = 8400.
Check.	I can check by multiplying 400 by 20 in a different order and then adding 400 to the answer.

Hints and tips

When multiplying or dividing multiples of 10, 100 or 1000, treat the numbers like single-digit whole numbers first, then multiply or divide by 10, 100 or 1000.

Questions

 1

a) On a computer game, Lee scores 300 points in Round 1. In Round 2 he scores 400 times more than in Round 1. How many points does he score in Round 2?

b) On his favourite computer game, Jamie scores 6000 points in Round 1 and 500 points in Round 2. His sister scores 3000 points in Round 1 and 900 points in Round 2. How many more points does Jamie score than his sister?

2

a) Josh scores 600 points in Round 1. In Round 2, he scores 500 times more than in Round 1. How many does he score in Rounds 1 and 2 together?

b) Helen scores 3000 points in Round 1. In Round 2, she scores 500 times less than in Round 1. Her brother scores 600 points in Round 1 and 700 points in Round 2. How many more points than her brother does Helen score altogether?

CHALLENGE.

Clive has these cards showing digits and signs.

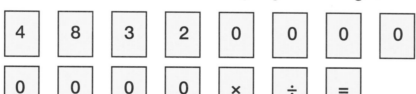

Make as many true statements as you can using the digit and operation cards above.

Explore

Find out about what children used to do for fun during the Second World War 70 years ago. Computers had not been invented. Go to **www.bbc.co.uk/schools/primaryhistory/world_war2/children_at_war/** and other websites that tell you about what toys children used to play with. Write an information sheet or web page about what you have found out.

Money

Questions about money can involve adding, subtracting, multiplying or dividing. Some may involve using a calculator.

Some football stickers cost 95p each. What is the maximum number of stickers I can buy with £17.32?

Read the question, now read it again.	Read slowly and carefully. Are the amounts in pounds or pence?
Decide your operations and units.	I'll work in pounds. I need to calculate 17.32 ÷ 0.95 and then I may have to round the answer *down* to the nearest whole number of stickers.
Approximate your answer.	95p is about £1, so I think the answer will be about 17 as there are 17 lots of £1 in £17.
Calculate.	17.32 ÷ 0.95 = 18.231579 Rounded down, the answer is 18 stickers.
Check.	I can check by multiplying 95p by 18 to check it is less than 1732p. Yes, it is 22p less, so I must be right.

Hints and tips

When you use a calculator for money questions, be careful to interpret the screen properly and round the answer if necessary so that it makes sense.

Questions

You can use your calculator to help you answer these questions.

1 a) Jack buys a football scarf for £8.60, three 95p stickers and a pair of football shorts for £11.99. How much change does he get from £30?

b) Football club shin pads cost £4.80 each. What is the maximum number of shin pads that can be bought with £30?

c) The price of a child's football shirt is $\frac{4}{5}$ of the price of an adult's shirt. Use a calculator to find the price of a child's football shirt if an adult's shirt costs £34.65.

2 a) A football club is advertising a special offer of 'Buy 2, get 1 free' on footballs. A football costs £9.29. A school spends £74.32 on footballs. How many balls will they get free?

b) How many footballs will the school get altogether?

c) At a different club, the price of a child's shirt is $\frac{5}{6}$ of the price of the adult's shirt. Use a calculator to find the price of the adult's football shirt if the child's shirt costs £11.55.

CHALLENGE!

Visit some online football club shops and find prices of different items. Write some questions about the information you find for a partner to solve. Don't forget to work out the answers!

Explore

A picture of Charles Darwin is printed on English £10 notes. Who was he? Find out more about him and why he is famous.

Negative numbers

Negative numbers are those that are lower or less than zero. We use negative numbers for cold temperatures, e.g. −4°C or −10°C, and for numbers below zero on a number line or below ground or sea level.

A skyscraper has 24 floors above ground level and 6 basement floors below ground. The floors are numbered from 24 down to −6, with 0 being ground level. The lift is at Level 14. It goes down 18 floors. What number floor is it at now?

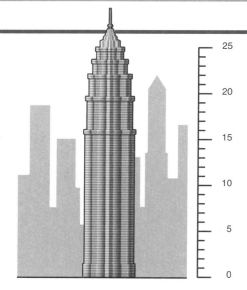

Read the question, now read it again.

Read slowly and carefully. Can I use the number line to help me?

Decide your operations and units.

I look at the number line and jump down 18 jumps from 14.

Approximate your answer.

If I jump down 14 from 14 I still have 4 more down to jump.

Calculate.

$14 - 18 = -4$
The lift will be at floor −4.

Check.

I count up 18 floors from −4 to check I reach 14. Yes!

Hints and tips

Be careful to count the jumps as you move up and down the number line.

Questions

 1
a) The lift is at floor −3 and it goes up 10 floors. Which floor is it at now?

b) The lift is at floor 8 and it goes down 13 floors. Which floor is it at now?

c) The lift is at floor −6 and it goes up 4 floors. Which floor is it at now?

2
a) Starting at floor 20, the lift goes down 25 floors and then up 7 floors. Which floor is it at now?

b) Starting at floor −3, the lift goes up 16 floors, down 9 floors and then up 12 floors. Which floor is it at now?

c) Starting at floor 13, the lift goes down 6 floors, down 9 floors, down 3 floors and then up 20 floors. Which floor is it at now?

CHALLENGE!

Write three problems of your own like this for a partner to solve. Remember to work out the answers too, so you can check your partner's calculations!

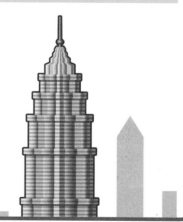

Explore

Find out about the tallest buildings in the world. In which countries are they, how tall are they and how many floors do they have? Design a poster about what you find out.

Reading scales

When solving some word problems you may need to read a scale and then add, subtract, multiply or divide.

Look at the amounts of water in these containers.

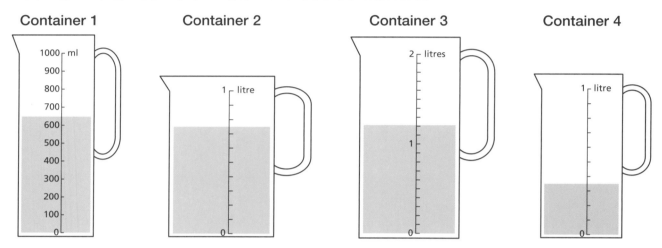

Container 1   Container 2   Container 3   Container 4

If 125 ml is poured out of container 3, how many millilitres of water will be left?

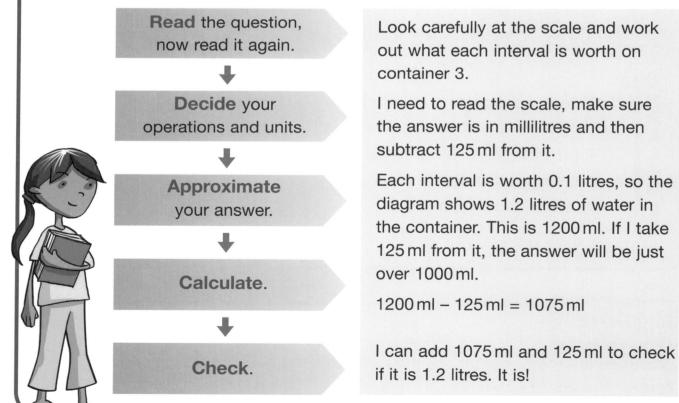

Read the question, now read it again.

⬇

Decide your operations and units.

⬇

Approximate your answer.

⬇

Calculate.

⬇

Check.

Look carefully at the scale and work out what each interval is worth on container 3.

I need to read the scale, make sure the answer is in millilitres and then subtract 125 ml from it.

Each interval is worth 0.1 litres, so the diagram shows 1.2 litres of water in the container. This is 1200 ml. If I take 125 ml from it, the answer will be just over 1000 ml.

1200 ml – 125 ml = 1075 ml

I can add 1075 ml and 125 ml to check if it is 1.2 litres. It is!

Hints and tips

To find the value of each interval on a scale, count how many spaces there are between numbered marks. Divide the difference between the numbers marked by the number of spaces. For example, in the first scale on container 1 opposite there are 10 spaces between 0 and 1000. The difference between 0 and 1000 ml is 1000 ml, so divide 1000 ml by 10 to get 100 ml. Each interval is worth 100 ml.

Questions

Look at the containers on page 32.

1

a) Find the difference, in millilitres, between the amounts of water in container 1 and container 2.

b) Find the difference, in millilitres, between the largest and smallest amounts in the four containers.

c) Find the total amount of liquid, in litres, in the two jugs that are holding the most.

2

a) Which three of the containers hold $1\frac{3}{4}$ litres altogether?

b) If the liquid in container 2 is poured into three smaller containers, so that each holds the same amount, how many millilitres would be in each?

c) Find the total amount of liquid in all the containers.

CHALLENGE!

Joe pours half the juice from this jug into a glass. He then adds 150 ml of water and drinks half of the mixture. How much of the mixture is left in the glass?

Explore

Make up your own fruit juice recipes. Use your favourite juices and write out how much of each you think it might need. Write a set of instructions and draw a picture of the finished drink.

Measures (1)

When solving mass problems you may need to add, subtract, multiply or divide. Always change the measurements so that they are in either grams or kilograms when answering.

Kylie receives four presents for her birthday.

Present A	**Present B**	**Present C**	**Present D**

$\frac{3}{4}$ kg	400 g	0.6 kg	1.25 kg

Present C is a pair of trainers in a box. If the box weighs 100 g, how much does each trainer weigh?

Read the question, now read it again.	How much is 0.6 kg? It is the same as 600 g.
Decide your operations and units.	I need to take 100 g from 600 g and divide the answer by 2.
Approximate your answer.	$600 \div 2 = 300$ so each trainer will weigh less than 300 g.
Calculate.	$600 - 100 = 500$; $500 \div 2 = 250$ g Each trainer weighs 250 g.
Check.	I can add 250 g, 250 g and 100 g to see if it is 0.6 kg. It is!

Hints and tips

Remember that 1000 grams (1000 g) is the same as one kilogram (1 kg).

Questions

1 **a)** Kylie picks up present C in her left hand and present A in her right hand. What is the difference in mass between the two presents?

b) What is the difference in mass between the heaviest and the lightest presents?

c) What is the mass of all four presents in total, in kilograms?

2 **a)** There are three identical mugs inside present A, each in their own box. Each box weighs 50 g. What is the mass of one of the mugs?

b) Present B is a large box of chocolates containing 40 chocolates. The empty box weighs 80 g. What is the average mass of each chocolate?

CHALLENGE! Make up three present questions of your own for a partner to solve. Check their answers.

Explore

In some countries and cultures birthdays are not celebrated, but other occasions are. In Greece it is the custom to celebrate 'name days', when everyone else with the same name as you also celebrates. For example, the name day for everyone called Andreas or Andrea is November 30th. Can you find out the dates for other names?

Measures (2)

When solving problems about measures you need to be careful to use the correct units. For these questions, you may use a calculator to help you work out the answers.

On a 330 ml can of cola it says that for each 100 ml of cola there are 42 calories.
How many calories are in the whole can?
Round your answer to the nearest whole number.

Read the question, now read it again.

Decide your operations and units.

Approximate your answer.

Calculate.

Check.

Read carefully. Think about what you are being asked to do.

I'll see how many lots of 100 ml are in 330 ml by dividing 330 by 100 and then I'll multiply 42 calories by that number and then round.

330 is about 3 times larger than 100; 3 × 40 = 120 calories.

330 ml ÷ 100 ml = 3.3; 42 × 3.3 = 138.6 calories.
Rounded to the nearest whole number this is 139 calories.

I can divide 138.6 by 42 to check it is 3.3.

Hints and tips

Remember that 1000 grams (1000 g) is the same as one kilogram (1 kg) and 1000 millilitres (1000 ml) is the same as 1 litre (1 l).

Questions

For these problems, use a calculator and round up the answers to the next whole number.

1

a) A can holds 330 ml of cola. How much less than one litre do two cans hold?

b) Kim buys six 2-litre bottles of cola and twelve 330 ml cans of cola for a party. How many litres of cola does she have altogether?

c) In every 100 ml of cola there are 10.6 g of carbohydrate. How much carbohydrate is in a 330 ml can?

2

a) On a 3.5 litre bottle of cola it says that for each 100 ml of cola there are 42 calories. How many calories are there in the whole bottle?

b) Six cans of cola together weigh 2.1 kg, including the mass of the cans themselves. If 330 g of each can is the cola, what is the actual mass of one empty can?

c) On a bottle of cola it says that a 250 ml serving contains 26.5 g of sugar. How much sugar is there in a 2-litre bottle?

CHALLENGE!

Find the nutritional information for a can or bottle of a different drink, such as orange juice or lemonade. Write some questions of your own for a partner to answer about the information. Don't forget to work out the answers too!

Explore

Did you know that Coca Cola was invented in 1886 by a pharmacist? Can you find out his name? Did you know that each day one billion Coca Colas are consumed! Look on the Internet for more about the history of the drink and try writing one billion using digits.

Time

Some time problems involve reading times in 24-hour digital form and using the information to answer questions.

Sheena is travelling by train from London to Newcastle. The first clock shows the time the train leaves London and the second clock shows the time the train arrives in Newcastle. How long is the journey?

Read the question, now read it again.

⬇

Decide your operations and units.

⬇

Approximate your answer.

⬇

Calculate.

⬇

Check.

Read carefully and look at the clocks. What do you need to do?

14:48 is the same as 2:48 p.m. and 18:35 is the same as 6:35 p.m. I must count on from 2:48 to 6:35 to find the journey length.

From 2:40 to 6:40 is 4 hours, so it'll be less than 4 hours.

The answer is 3 hours + 12 mins + 35 mins = 3 hours 47 mins.

I can count back 3 hours 47 mins from 18:35 to make sure.

Hints and tips

A 24-hour clock shows the hours between midday and midnight using the numbers 12–23. Subtract 12 from the hour to find the time in 12-hour form. When solving time problems count on, or back, to the nearest whole hour to make your calculation easier. Never just add numbers because this will give you the wrong answer.

Questions

1 a) This clock shows the time a train leaves Manchester. It arrives in Leeds at 16:10. How long is the journey?

`15:29`

b) A train arrives at York station at 13:56 and leaves the station 24 minutes later. What time does it leave the station?

c) A train takes 35 minutes to get from Scarborough to Malton. It arrives at Malton at 19:18. What time does it leave Scarborough?

2 a) A night train leaves London at 22:43 and arrives in Edinburgh at 07:20 the next day. How long is the journey?

b) Sanjiv takes 7 hours and 29 minutes to get from Liverpool to Bournemouth by train. He leaves Liverpool at 10:16 in the morning. What time does he arrive in Bournemouth? Give your answer in 24-hour form.

c) Jane takes a train from Birmingham to Scarborough, but has to change trains at York. The total journey takes 5 hours and 17 minutes, plus a 22 minute stop in York. She leaves Birmingham at 08:03. What time does she arrive in Scarborough? Give your answer in 24-hour form.

CHALLENGE!

Go to www.thetrainline.com and enter the name of a station near you and somewhere else you'd like to go. Find out the train times and work out the length of the journey. Record your findings in a fact sheet.

Explore

Find out about the famous engineer, George Stephenson, known as the 'Father of Railways'. He designed and built the steam railways in the 1800s. Create a video of what you have found out.

2-D and 3-D shapes

When solving 2-D and 3-D shape problems you need to remember the names of common shapes and their properties, such as how many sides, faces, edges, vertices (corners), or right angles or lines of symmetry they have.

One face of each of these 3-D shapes is shaded.

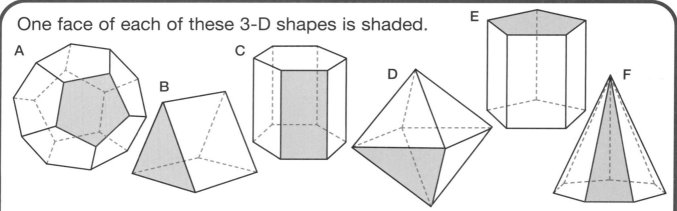

Shape A is a dodecahedron. How many faces does the dodecahedron have, what is the name of the shape of the shaded face and is the shaded face regular or not?

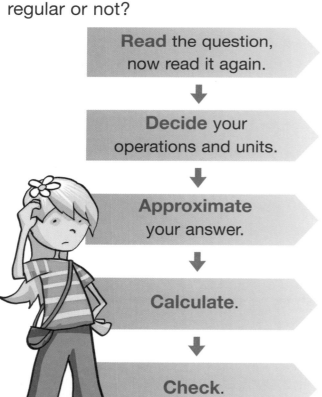

Read the question, now read it again.	Read slowly and carefully. You are being asked three questions.
Decide your operations and units.	I need to count the faces and work out what shape the shaded face is, including whether it is regular or not.
Approximate your answer.	I'll imagine I was holding this shape in my hands.
Calculate.	I think the shape has 12 faces. The shaded face has five equal sides and five equal angles so it is a regular pentagon.
Check.	I'll check that I've answered all parts of the question.

Hints and tips

A regular 2-D shape is one that has equal sides and equal angles. A regular triangle is called an equilateral triangle.

Questions

1 a) Shape D is a tetrahedron. How many faces does the tetrahedron have, what is the name of the shape of the shaded face and is the shaded face regular or not?

b) Look at shape B. What is the name of the 3-D shape? Two of its faces are triangles, what are the names of the shapes of the other faces and how many are there?

2 a) Fin chooses one of the shapes shown. It has a face that is a regular hexagon. Which shape is it and what is the name of its shaded face?

b) A shape is made from the following faces: one regular quadrilateral and four equilateral triangles. What is the name of the shape?

CHALLENGE! Look around you and find boxes and objects that are different 3-D shapes. Make a list of these shapes, the shapes of their faces and their properties. E.g.:

A Toblerone bar is a triangular prism, with two faces that are equilateral triangles and three rectangular faces. The rectangles are not regular.

Explore

3-D shapes that have all straight edges are known as **polyhedrons**. These shapes appear in lots of computer-generated art. Go to Google images and search for 'polyhedron art' and choose your favourite images. You could try drawing your own designs or could copy your favourites.

Angles

An angle is an amount of turn and is measured in degrees. When answering problems about angles, always use the degree symbol (°) in your answers, e.g. 90°.

The minute hand on a clock turns through 360° in one hour, 180° in half an hour and 90° in quarter of an hour. Through how many degrees does the minute hand turn between 12:10 and 12:55?

Read the question, now read it again.

Decide your operations and units.

Approximate your answer.

Calculate.

Check.

Read slowly and carefully. Through how much of a full turn has the hand turned?

The difference between 12:55 and 12:10 is 45 minutes or $\frac{3}{4}$ hr. The answer will be three times larger than the angle it turns in $\frac{1}{4}$ hr.

It is more than half an hour, 180°, and less than a whole hour, 360°.

$3 \times 90° = 270°$

I can check by adding 90° to 180° to see if it is 270°. Yes, I'm right!

Hints and tips

Remember that the minute hand turns through 360° in one hour, 180° in half an hour and 90° in quarter of an hour.

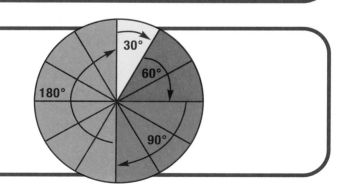

Questions

1
a) Through how many degrees does the minute hand of a clock turn between 1:05 p.m. and 1:35 p.m.?

b) Jim looks at his watch at 6:55 a.m. and then at 7:10 a.m. Through what angle has the minute hand of his watch turned?

c) The minute hand of a clock turns through what angle between 11:05 a.m. and 11:50 a.m.?

2
a) Through how many degrees does the minute hand turn between 4:20 p.m. and 4:25 p.m.?

b) Julia starts eating at 12:50 p.m. and finishes at 1:10 p.m. Through what angle does the minute hand of her watch turn while she eats?

c) Through how many degrees does the minute hand of a clock turn between 7:25 a.m. and 8:15 a.m.?

CHALLENGE!

Find out what angle the minute hand of a watch turns through during one minute.

Explore

The Ancient Egyptians are said to have worked out a way of making right angles, using a length of rope with knots tied along it. The knots were equally spaced along the rope and there were 10 knots. Two of the knots were held together by one person and two others pulled two of the other knots, so that the rope made a right-angled triangle. Find out more about this or try it yourself with some string, a ruler and a pen to mark where the knots should be.

Data handling

Data handling questions will ask you to look at a graph, chart or table and use the data to answer the questions.

Here is a frequency chart showing the different ways children in Year 5 celebrated their birthday with friends.

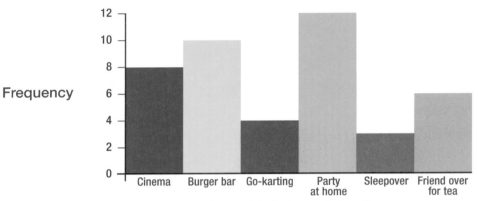

How many children in Year 5 celebrated their birthday by going go-karting?

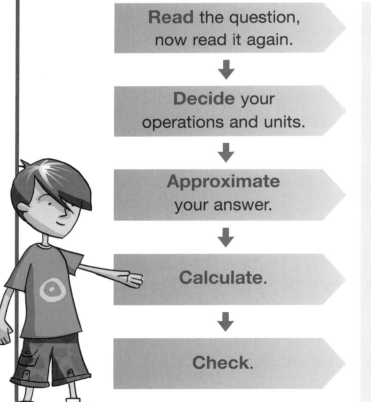

Read the question, now read it again.	Read slowly and carefully. What are you being asked to do?
Decide your operations and units.	The chart is telling me how the Year 5 children celebrate their birthday.
Approximate your answer.	I have to look at the column labelled 'Go-karting' (dark blue).
Calculate.	The height of the column labelled 'Go-karting' shows the answer: 4 children.
Check.	I can double check my answer to make sure I was correct.

Hints and tips

Look at the titles of the graph and the axes first. They tell you what information the graph is trying to show.

Questions

1 a) How many children in Year 5 chose to have a party at home?

b) Which was the least popular way of celebrating a birthday?

c) How many children in total either went to a burger bar or the cinema?

2 a) How many more children went to a burger bar than had a sleepover?

b) Which was more popular; staying at home in some form or going out. By how many?

c) What is the total number of children that took part in the survey?

CHALLENGE!

Using a computer either at home or at school, copy and paste the league table of your favourite football team onto a new document. Then write your own word problems based on the information given in the table. You can find most football league tables in the sport section of the BBC website.

Explore

The Ancient Egyptians gathered data about the level of the River Nile flood waters each year. This meant they could predict the amount of food they could grow and therefore how much tax their government could collect. Investigate Ancient Egyptian agriculture and make an information sheet from your findings.

Answers

Sequences
(Pages 10–11)
Questions:
1 a) 59, 77
  b) 37, 20
  c) 47, 50, 63
2 a) 3.2, 2.4
  b) 1.0, 1.7, 2.4

Mixed calculations (1)
(Pages 12–13)
Questions:
1 a) 358 passengers
  b) 173 passengers
  c) 7 passengers
2 a) 284 seats
  b) 89 empty seats
  c) 14 seats per row

Mixed calculations (2)
(Pages 14–15)
Questions:
1 a) 5967 votes
  b) 223 men
2 a) 564 votes
  b) 2223 votes

Fractions
(Pages 16–17)
Questions:
1 a) $\frac{3}{5}$
  b) $\frac{3}{10}$
  c) $\frac{1}{5}$
2 a) $\frac{2}{3}$
  b) $\frac{7}{8}$

Decimals
(Pages 18–19)
Questions:
1 a) Eva by 0.05 kg
  b) 46.35 kg
  c) 45.65 kg
2 a) 85.06 kg, 85.35 kg, 85.6 kg, 85.62 kg, 86 kg
  b) Eva 43.5 kg; Ivor 130.5 kg

Percentages
(Pages 20–21)
Questions:
1 a) 60%
  b) 73%
  c) 24%
2 a) 80%
  b) 10%
  c) 7%

Equivalence
(Pages 22–23)
Questions:
1 a) $\frac{3}{4}$, 0.75, 75%
  b) $\frac{1}{4}$, 0.25, 25%
  c) 2
2 a) $\frac{1}{2}$, 0.5, 50%
  b) $\frac{5}{8}$
  c) 33%
Challenge:
Approx 17%

Ratio
(Pages 24–25)
Questions:
1 a) 20 girls
  b) 18 boys
  c) 9 girls
2 a) 20 boys, 4 girls
  b) 12 boys, 16 girls
Challenge:
4:5 8:10 12:15 16:30 and so on

Place value
(Pages 26–27)
Questions:
1 a) 120 000
  b) 2600
2 a) 1700
  b) 4200

Money
(Pages 28–29)
Questions:
1 a) £6.56
  b) 6 shin pads
  c) £27.72
2 a) 4 free balls
  b) 12 footballs
  c) £13.86

Negative numbers
(Pages 30–31)
Questions:
1 a) floor 7
   b) floor –5
   c) floor –2
2 a) floor 2
   b) floor 16
   c) floor 15

Reading scales
(Pages 32–33)
Questions:
1 a) 100 ml
   b) 850 ml
   c) 1.95 l
2 a) containers 1, 2 and 4
   b) 250 ml
   c) 2.95 l

Measures (1)
(Pages 34–35)
Questions:
1 a) 0.15 kg
   b) 0.85 kg
   c) 3 kg
2 a) 200 g
   b) 8 g

Measures (2)
(Pages 36–37)
Questions:
1 a) 340 ml
   b) 16 l
   c) 35 g
2 a) 1470 calories
   b) 20 g
   c) 212 g

Time
(Pages 38–39)
Questions:
1 a) 41 mins
   b) 14:20
   c) 18:43
2 a) 8 hours 37 minutes
   b) 17:45
   c) 13:42

2-D and 3-D shapes
(Pages 40–41)
Questions:
1 a) 8, triangle, regular
   b) triangular prism, square or rectangle, 3
2 a) C, rectangle
   b) square-based pyramid

Angles
(Pages 42–43)
Questions:
1 a) 180°
   b) 90°
   c) 270°
2 a) 30°
   b) 120°
   c) 300°
Challenge:
6°

Data handling
(Pages 44–45)
Questions:
1 a) 12 children
   b) sleepover
   c) 18 children
2 a) 7 more
   b) going out by 1
   c) 43

Notes